5/6 F's Perpetual, Purposeful, Perfect Poetry

Year Five/Six F Albany Rise P. S.

BookLeaf Publishing

5/6 F's Perpetual, Purposeful, Perfect Poetry

Presentation by *BookLeaf Publishing*

Web: www.bookleafpub.com

E-mail: info@bookleafpub.com

ISBN: 978-93-95784-13-9

First edition 2022

DEDICATION

Us, and young children across the world. You're all capable of anything you set your mind to.

ACKNOWLEDGEMENT

We would like to acknowledge our families, friends and teachers for all your hard work and guidance to making us who we are today.

PREFACE

A range of poems, including limericks, acrostics, couplets and ones with so much alliteration your tongue will struggle to stay on.

Themes...for you to find out.

My Emotions

Hi, I'm Jun Qi (Joon-chi). My best friends are like a triangle, two are acute and one is very obtuse. My friends are vast and open but very soon they'll become a very miserable omen.

My life is like a scary ride. There's ups and downs, lefts and rights but life is most scary in fight.

My school purpose is not what I desired because I have been used by many, many, many students which make me especially tired.

My future path is unclear. Maybe I'll be near my friends or I'll have many huge dents. So many conclusions and so many paths to lose but so far none to use.

I'm very confused, confused, confused. "Why must I have so much to remember and lose?"

Chorus Dark to Light

The darkness will come,
The darkness will come,
The darkness will come to devour me,
The songs will not sing,
The light will not shine,
Because I will be gone by the time this song rhymes,
The light will soon shine,
The songs will be sung,
For this little bird has flown to the sun.

The Frightening Roller Coaster Ride

Whoosh went the roller coaster with a zip and a zap, crashing through the water.
Bump, flying through the sky.
Thump back on the frightening tracks.

The Randomness Poem

There is a man who owns a van,
He loves to eat sand on demand.
The man saw a cat that ate a hat,
after that the cat got fat.
It was a ride but his card declined,
He went to sleep whilst counting sheep.

Bills = Ill

I had a bill,
but then I got ill.
I stayed in my room,
for days and days.
But then I got out,
It was like a maze,
Beacause of the nasty haze.

The dog on a walk

The dog was on a walk,
His owner had a talk.
His secretary got a mop,
and she thought...
"Did you the dog pour...
The water on the floor?"
I'm going to the store!
Be careful of the wild boar!

Shrek

Shrek lives in a swamp.
He's so lonely, except he has a friend called Tony but his friend called Tony was just made of boloney, so Shrek was sad and mad. Shrek went out and stole a water spout, The cops came for Shrek and when he was running they found his uncle Beck.

Lightning and Thunder

Boom! Crash!
The sounds of terror and thunder followed by a beam of burning lights. Sounds of horror scare all creatures big and small, and it has not been tamed by the lightening fame.

The electric shocks rushing through your veins. Paralysing or burning everything it touches. Bright lights crash into trees and objects setting fire to surrounding victims.

Angry vs Sad

ANGRY
Furious, Frustrated
Lurking, Roaming, Uncontrollable
Mad, Ungrateful, Disappointed, Moody
Lurking, Stressing, Disturbing
Moody, Unhappy
SAD

Autumn to Spring

Autumn
Cold, breeze
Falling, shivering, raining
Wind, leaves, picnic, fruit
Growing, warming, shining
Warm, pool
Spring

The funny old cat with a hat

There once was a funny old cat with a mat, who would always wear a flat hat. He loved to walk and also talk. That funny old cat with a hat. After that, the cat ate a rat that was very, very fat.

Home against School

School
Boring, Scary
Writing, Reading, Running
Work, Books, Relax, Fun
Sleeping, Chilling, Eating
Comfortable, Amazing,
Home!

Autumn VS Spring

Autumn
Cloudy, Cold
Shivering, Falling, Raining
Orange, Leaves, Flowers, Sunny
Blooming, Boiling, Swimming
Bright, lushes
Spring

The Ninjas

Crime - fighters
Stealth - slicers
Mission - completers

Sword - welders
Shuriken - throwers
Sneaky - trespassers

Great Halloween Eve

Ohh! Ahh! Boom! Crash!
The thunder and lightning clap. In the depths of the creepy park, lays a freaky man on Halloweens Eve.
He's back from the dead.
His name is Steve...
A kid said 'Why does he bleed?' 'Why is he green?'
He then replied, 'I...am....Steve!'

Summer's fall

Summer
Bluest of skies, hottest of weather
Laughing, swimming, enjoying
Happy, beach, hail, wind
Falling, shivering, freezing
Cloudy, cool
Autumn!

Blue Monkey

Brilliant blue bananas
Luscious luxurious jungle
United animal kingdom
Egotistical animals

Mindless manoeuvres
Octagonal hairy heads
Nigerian tree climbers
Kinetic cake eaters
Economic egg eaters
Yellow smelling fruits

World where monsters live

There was a world where monsters lived in the darkness where the world was engulfed by black and the screeches ruled this land. Monsters that devoured everything in sight, but are you willing to start a fight?
Although you might be able to fight, nothing will stand the mighty hand.
Will you fight the hand, pull your sword up and make a stand?
Free this world from its endless despair.
Be the hero that we need in this land.
Take my hand, explore this land, for you are very rare.

Monkeys

Monkeys live in jungles,
Originated in South America.
Nigerian banana eaters,
Korean tree climbers.
Eyes blue,
Yellow is rare.
South American proud invention!

Socks

2 socks make a pair,
he washed them fair and square,
The socks were revolting that he wanted them to sparkle after some time,
they were then as clean as a dime.

The Witch

Whizzing in the night sky,
in and out, she flies around,
tightly holding on to her broomstick,
casting her magical spells,
hiding in the dark sky.

www.ingramcontent.com/pod-product-compliance
Lightning Source LLC
Chambersburg PA
CBHW051716130826
49812CB00034B/1217
* 9 7 8 9 3 9 5 7 8 4 1 3 9 *